Other works:

By Other Authors About Touchy:

The Fight For Golden Dawn - Jessie P. Terwilliger (Paperback, Kindle)

Touchy The Clown Series:

Touchy Kills A Lady Bug   (Paperback)
Touchy Goes To Hollywood (Paperback, Kindle)
Touchy Goes To Washington   (Paperback, Kindle)
Touchy Goes To Jail   (Out Of Print)
Touchy Saves The World   (Coming Summer of 2020)
Touchy Goes Catphishing   (Brick & Mortar ONLY)
Touchy And The MILF Next Door   (Paperback, Kindle)

Apotheosis Series:

Sorest Rump Or: How I Changed The World (Paperback)

The Book Of Stuart Or: Sleeping Beauty & The Beast & The Path Of Christ's Return (Paperback)

Umbrance Or: Don't Bother, You Wouldn't Understand; And You Can't Afford It Anyway!!! (Paperback)

TV, Film & Commercials:

(See if you can Catch a Glimpse of Touchy & His Antics)

General Hospital	Awkward
My Name Is Earl	Pretty Little Liars
Bones	Workaholics
Cold Case Files	The Mentalist
Ant Farm	Criminal Minds
The Office	GLEE
It's Always Sunny In Philadelphia	Gates
Clear History	The Bachelor
Love, Victor	Blackish
American Horror Story	And Many Many More...
HEROS	
The Young & The Restless	
Son's Of Anarchy	
Tosh.0	
NASCAR Super Bowl Spot	
Modern Family	
The Middle	
DEXTER (Who ironically failed twice to notice Touchy)	
Keeping Up With the Kardashians	

<u>To Dylan:</u>

You really should answer your phone!

One
basic
truth can
be used as
a foundation for
a mountain of lies,
and if we dig down deep
enough in the mountain of lies,
and bring out that truth, to set it
on top of the mountain of lies; the entire
mountain of lies will crumble under the weight of
that one truth, and there is nothing more devastating to a
structure of lies than the revelation of the truth upon which
the structure of lies was built, because the shock waves of
the revelation of the truth reverberate, and continue to
reverberate throughout the Earth for generations to
follow, awakening even those
people who had no
desire to be
awakened
to the
truth.

Delamer Duverus

"You can't build a reputation on what
you're *going* to do"
Henry Ford

If you are
planning for a year,
plant a garden;
if you are
planning for 20 years,
<u>Plant Trees;</u>
if you are
planning for **100 years,**
Teach The Children!

-Chinese proverb

"Time we put some Real Clowns in the
White House."
Touchy The Clown

"The only Card that Trumps Trump is
The Joker!"
@RexOfTheWorld

"Nobody's Ridin' With Biden"
Black Touchy

"Ask not what your country can do for
you: Ask what Stu can do for your
country!!!"
Touchy The Clown

In The Beginning was The Code; and The Code was with The Programer: and The Code WAS The Programmer.

Authorized King Richard Stuart Version
The Book of John
Chapter 1 Verse 1

11 And I saw Heaven Opened, and Behold a White Horse; and He that sat upon him was called Faithful and True, and in Righteousness He doth Judge and Make War. 12 His eyes were as a Flame of Fire, and on His head were Many Crowns; and He had a Name Written, that no man knew, but He Himself. 13 And He was clothed with a Vesture dipped in Blood: and His name is called The Word of God. 14 And the Armies which were in Heaven followed Him upon white horses, clothed in fine linen, white and clean. 15 And out of His Mouth goeth a Sharp Sword, that with it He should Smite the Nations: and He Shall Rule Them With A Rod Of Iron: and he treadeth the winepress of the fierceness and wrath of Almighty God. 16 And he hath on his Vesture and on his thigh a name written: KING OF KINGS, & LORD OF LORDS.

King James Stuart Version
The Book of Revelation
Chapter 19:11-16

Uncle Touchy's

Ad Ventures In Candyland

By:

Richard Lee Stuart Jr.

Uncle Touchy's Ad Ventures

In

<u>Candyland</u>

Touchy The Clown

had a

secret!

Touchy was a Clown

who was Born

to

Wear a Crown;

but he didn't want

The People

to know *that* yet either...

Touchy The Clown

Had

A

Mission:

PROTECT

THE

CHILDREN

Touchy The Clown
Once had friends named:
Donny & Crystal

The First Time Touchy's Carnival
BOOKED IN
Candyland Abusments
Crystal pointed at the owner's nephew
Sweet Dick Jones
And said:
"He Raped me!"

Crystal was only 15 years old!

Touchy The Clown

Spent the next several seasons

working on his plan

to infiltrate

The Show

&

Find justice for His friend.

Little did He know

that he was

going down a rabbit hole

that would find him

at the

Center

of a

Satanic Network

Of

Pedophiles

&

Slave Owners

Touchy The Clown owned his own
business:
Airlusions Airbrushing
Touchy used to paint swimsuits onto
exotic dancers for clubs like
Deja Vu
&
Spearmint Rhino

Touchy also would paint faces &
temporary tattoos at carnivals and street
fairs.

Touchy could choose which Shows and
Events to play.

Touchy used this to his
advantage-making many friends ON
many shows…and hearing lots of
stories about many foes…

Touchy was able
to book in with
Candyland
For
ClearChannel's
Winter Wonderland
at The Verizon(Irvine Meadows)
Amphitheater for an entire month.

He was able to get an inside idea of the
operation.

Touchy even stopped operating his
airbrush business so he could work the
games for Candyland.

Touchy would repeatedly work locations like:

Sherman Oaks Street Fair

Hermosa Beach Pier Festival

Redondo Beach Street Fair
Pacific Palisades

City of Commerce 4th of July
Montrose Oktoberfest

West Hollywood Pride Festival ON Sunset

And countless Schools & Churches…

Touchy told the owner's nephew
Sweet Dick Jones
That Touchy
Had Warrants
&
was a
Regestered Sex Offender

Sweet Dick Jones
Was not bothered
by this information
&
even helped conceal
this information
from others
Except
for when he used
the information
to manipulate
those around
Touchy.

Touchy would sleep in Sweet Dick Jones' room for the first several months working for Candyland.

One day Sweet Dick Jones' 8-year-old nephew put his hand ON Touchy's knee and in an English Accent said:

"You're acting like you want it-just lay back and I'll take care of everything!"

Touchy stood up and asked Sweet Dick Jones what was going ON.

Sweet Dick Jones laughed.

The Consessions Manager had an English Accent and was openly gay and Touchy thought he had been molesting the nephew. Touchy told everybody ON the Show who would listen…

Touchy had access to Sweet Dick Jones' computer and saw Child Pornography.

Touchy reached out to Sweet Dick Jones' baby momma who in turn contacted the FBI.

Baby Momma said she KNEW Sweet Dick Jones and Touchy had Tag Teamed an 11-year-old girl who worked for the Show.

Touchy quit that day.

Touchy The Clown decided to reattempt
infiltration even though his cover had
already been blown.

He approached The Owner and
obtained employment directly.

Whilst rebuilding a Ferris Wheel for
Calamigos Ranch
Home of the Malibu Cafe
Touchy came into contact with
The Nephew
And Said:
"The last time I saw you you tried giving
me head in Robert's voice!"
To which was replied in David Cariden's
lisp from Kill Bill 2:
"Little did Stuart know it was Uncle
Dylan the entire time…"
Darby & Paul Mac were there and heard
the whole thing!

Touchy realized
NONE of these people
saw anything wrong
with what
was going ON.

All Touchy could do
was wait and gather information.

It was during this time
Touchy discovered
he was a target
for revenge
by the
Pedophiles
for outing their activities.

Moreover, it was their intent
to **Entrap & Enslave**
Touchy The Clown
FOREVER!

Touchy took
Sweet Dick Jones
&
The Blueberry Lounge
to work at Calamigos
ON the way home
Sweet Dick Jones
pretended to lose his phone.

Touchy was
asked to call
his son
to ping the location.

The phone was found
by the entrance to the first tunnel
heading towards the 101.

But now Touchy had been texting the
Owner's Nephew's 11-year-old son.
The plot thickens…

Touchy was working
at the
City of Industry Expo
the following day
building a carnival set for AppleTV.

The crew wanted to go to lunch,
so they all piled into
Touchy's Limo.

Touchy entered the destination of a
Mexican restaurant and hit start ON
google maps.

Google Maps _lead Touchy in circles
through a neighborhood_ before arriving
at the destination.

His passengers asked _coyly_ as to why
he had driven the way he did.
Touchy knew his phone was hacked…

Touchy returned
to the Expo
to tear down
the carnival.
Sweet Dick Jones
put drugs
into the workers' water bottles
that gave everyone
insomnia and rapid heart rates.

Touchy was made to go up onto one of
the trailers with no ladder to drop the
marque.

Immediately upon reaching
the top
Sweet Dick Jones' son ran over
suddenly offering to
throw up unrequested water
bottles-something he had never done
before.

Touchy started getting ready for
The Neon Carnival
A few days later.

Back at Candyland Headquarters
Sweet Dick Jones asked Touchy to call
his son's phone again

.

Sweet Dick Jones held Touchy's phone
and his own while speaking to his son
ON speaker phone.

When Touchy got his phone back *all
previous text messages to his son had
been deleted.*

Now Touchy has a Google Voice
account and *hasn't deleted a single text*
in over 12 years.
Hacking phones is investigated by the
FBI

Touchy went to Coachella to set up
THE NEON CARNIVAL
While he was there his employees
began acting strangely.
Darby eventually revealed a plot to jump
Touchy. When they were done jumping
Touchy they were each going to get
$100 to kick him in the head.
The justification to the other show's 12
employees was to be the *deleted text
messages.*
Touchy was then to be loaded into a box
truck and bound and gagged and then
boiling hot water was to be poured onto
the back of his neck to cause a boil
while beating his legs and rear and
other graphic tortures not to be
mentioned here.

If he survived he was to become a slave
to the SHOW

Touchy gathered his employees and took them home where Darby continued to tell Touchy many secrets while Touchy video recorded and broadcast ON facebook Live.

Darby told Touchy that she felt sexually harrassed: she told Touchy that "Daddy" had told her to have sex with Touchy and then claim rape so that he could be fired. Darby eventually indicated that "Daddy" was the SHOW OWNER. She said they were passing her around like a prison bitch and that it was Touchy's fault for leaving her there.

Touchy didn't know until that moment that it was happening! Darby said she was asexual but did what she had to to get along and prove she can hang. Darby said she wants a shot at a normal life.

Touchy left his employees to their own devices while HE began work ON THIS VERY BOOK in hopes that something could be done in the event of his disappearance…or to prevent his disappearance all together.
Touchy skipped The Neon Carnival and commenced writing.
Since His undertaking many other things were brought to mind. Touchy remembered the story he was told about BH by Paul Mac:
One day, a person working in the ticket box pretended to be a 10-year-old boy and was messaging a carny working one of the rides called BH.

Touchy remember when BH came to CANDYLAND he had a huge boil on his neck that He was told by Sweet Dick Jones to ask BH about.

BH was forced to live at the storage
yard and pay for the employee porta
potty out of his paycheck.
When BH retired from Candyland
Touchy bought some property with him
near Joshua Tree.
The day after inking the deal with the
land company BH told Touchy he had
something to show him that was going
to freak him out.

BH took off his sock to reveal the bottom
was black from gangrene!

Touchy said:
"Get in the car-they are going to cut that
off!"

Two days later they removed the foot.
The next week they took his leg below
the knee.

BH was intimidated into not seeking medical attention by Sweet Dick Jones out of fear that those text messages would be shown to authorities.

BH doesn't know that the person he was texting was an adult who set him up. Touchy never got to read the messages so there is no way of telling if BH had actually *thought* he was talking to a child.

MediCAL paid for the operation instead of his worker's compensation.

This is not an isolated incident.

Touchy had avoided a similar fate, but His career at Candylad had come to an end…

Touchy The Clown
Had infiltrated the web.

It wasn't until Touchy understood the full
scope of the situation that it occurred to
Him that He hadn't yet reached the
center of the web.

Touchy had to commune with
The Mother Spider
To truly seek a remedy.

Luckily Touchy knew Her very well…
Her husband was in fact from
Bohemian Grove

Touchy's problem revolved around
The Mother Spider being the financier
behind Touchy's Persecution

The Mother Spider
Held all the contracts for Hollywood

Her Name Was ON EVERYTHING

She was mad at Touchy because he
made a joke about J Lo.

Touchy thought: If you are that
concerned about the words of a Clown
you probably shouldn't be running the
Circus!

Touchy thought: I'm-so-sure that I'm the
first person to ever make a joke about J
Lo's Butt…and she's actually going to
hear it…and it's going to offend her.

Touchy thought: **IT'S MY LIFE-
I CAN TALK ABOUT IT TOO!!!**

Touchy The Clown
Wanted
Justice To Be Served

Touchy contacted His Uncle
William K. Gamble
Who owned
Twelve Law Offices
In California and Two in Nevada

Touchy Signed A
Non-Publishing Agreement
And promised not to release
The Non-Fiction
Biography
Of
Candyland
Until After Everyone's Death
In Exchange
Touchy Would Receive
Per Diem for His Presidential Campaign

Touchy The Clown

Went

ON

to

Win

The White House

Sweet Dick Jones

Went To

Rehab

Darby

Got The Help

She Needed

Paul Mac

Got Some

New Shoes

The Kids Were

Finally Believed

Touchy The Clown
No Longer Had To Ignore
The Cries Of His Subjects

Touchy had established Himself in &
across multiple industries and His
friends were long trusted members of
several different Shows.

Touchy was always guarded by the most
downtrodden working amongst the rank
& file-they knew the truth & told him
What He Needed to Know
To
Save The Show!

The
Show
Must
Go
ON!!!